Amazing World of Ants

Written by Francene Sabin
Illustrated by Eulala Conner

Troll Associates

Library of Congress Cataloging in Publication Data

Sabin, Francene.
Amazing world of ants.

Summary: Describes the physical characteristics and behavior of ants.
1. Ants—Juvenile literature. [1. Ants] I. Conner, Eulala. II. Title.
QL568.F7S15 595.79'6 81-7492
ISBN 0-89375-558-3 AACR2
ISBN 0-89375-559-1 (pbk.)

Printed in the United States of America.

10 9 8 7 6 5 4 3 2

Picnics mean fresh air, playing games on the grass, tasty food—and ants. First one ant appears. Then three or four. Soon there are long lines of ants marching right to the food.

Ants are always busy looking for food. When one finds some, it tells other ants. It does this by tapping other ants with its *antennae* (an-*ten*-ee). Antennae are long, thin feelers that stick out of the top of an ant's head.

Ants are very neat insects. On each of an ant's two front legs there is a comb. An ant cleans its feelers by lifting a leg and drawing the feeler through the comb.

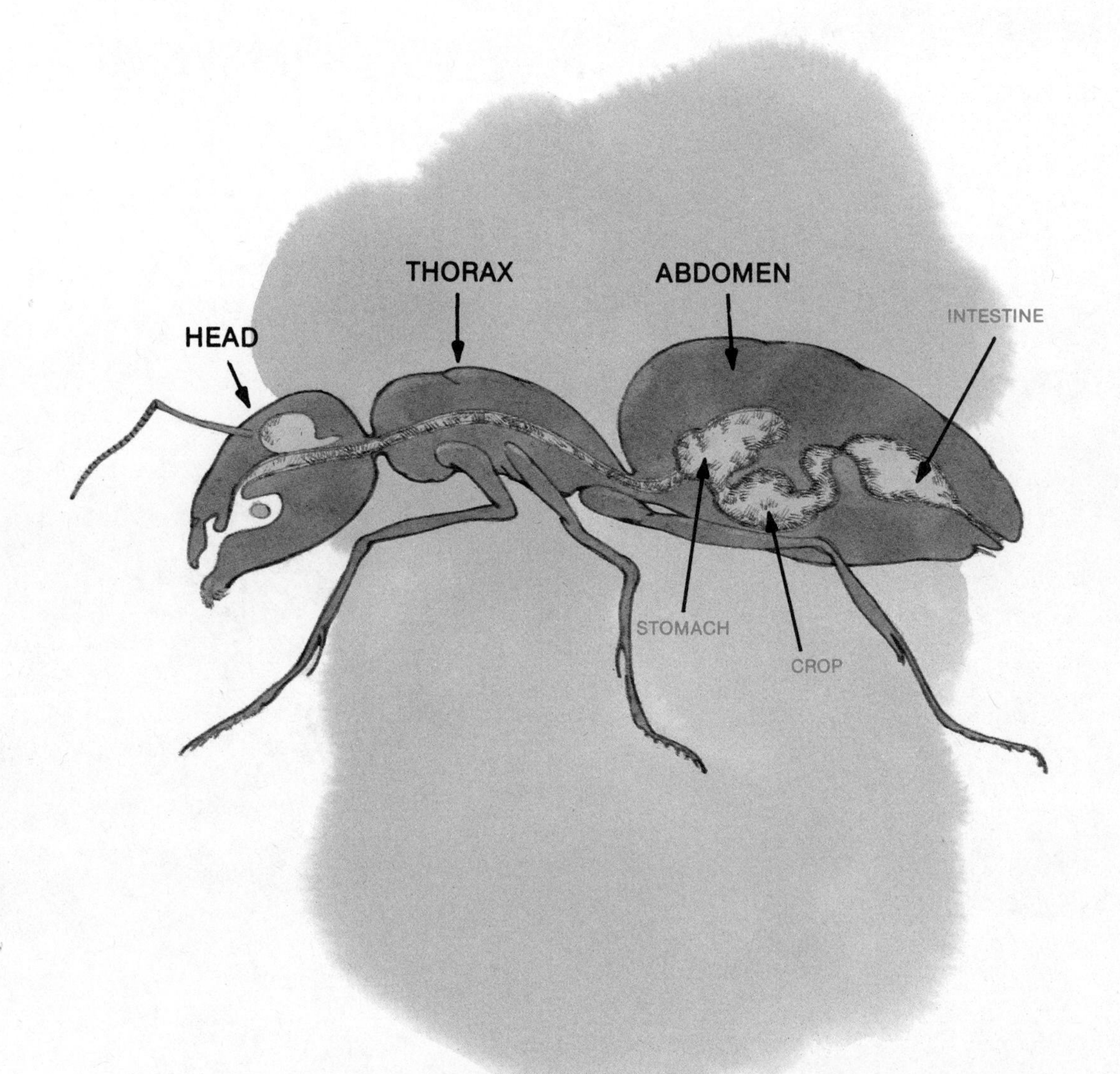

An ant's body has three parts. The head is in front. Behind the head is the middle part, called the *thorax*. The ant's six legs are connected to the thorax.

The back part of the ant is called the *abdomen*. The ant's *stomach*, *crop*, and *intestine* are in the abdomen.

When an ant eats, some of the food is stored in the crop. This food is brought up later by the ant to feed other ants in the nest. The rest of the food goes into the ant's stomach and intestine.

Ants also have a way to show other ants where food is. If an ant finds something to eat, it rushes back to the nest. On the way, it stops every few inches, pressing its abdomen to the ground. This leaves a trail of scents that will lead other ants to the food.

Ants live in groups called *colonies*. All the ants in a colony help each other and work together. They feed each other, and they fight for each other.

An ant colony lives in a nest. The ants dig this nest in the ground. Some ants spend their whole lives digging. They never leave the nest to look for food. These ants are fed by other ants, whose job it is to bring food to the colony.

An ant nest has many rooms. Some of the rooms are used to store food. Some of the rooms are used for ant eggs. There is a room just for the queen ant, too.

In every colony, there are at least three kinds of ants. They are the queen, the worker, and the drone. Some colonies also have soldier ants. Each type of ant has a job to do. Worker ants dig, hunt for food, and take care of the eggs.

Soldier ants protect the nest. They look just like worker ants, only a little larger. The drone is a small ant with wings. Drone ants have only one job—to mate with the queen.

The queen ant's job is to lay all the eggs. A queen ant lives many years and lays hundreds of eggs each year. The other ants in the nest bring food to the queen, protect her, and take care of the eggs. The queen is much larger than any other ant in the colony.

There are lots of things going on in an ant nest. Of course, all you can see is the opening on top of the ground, and maybe a few ants. But inside the colony, ants are busily at work in the rooms and tunnels of the nest.

In one room are the ant eggs. They are tiny—about the size of the dot over the letter “i”—and white. A worker ant takes care of the eggs, keeping them warm and moist. In about 24 days, the eggs will hatch and become *larvae* (*lar*-vee). Ant larvae look like tiny, fat, white worms. Workers take the larvae from the egg nursery to the larvae nursery where they are fed by other workers.

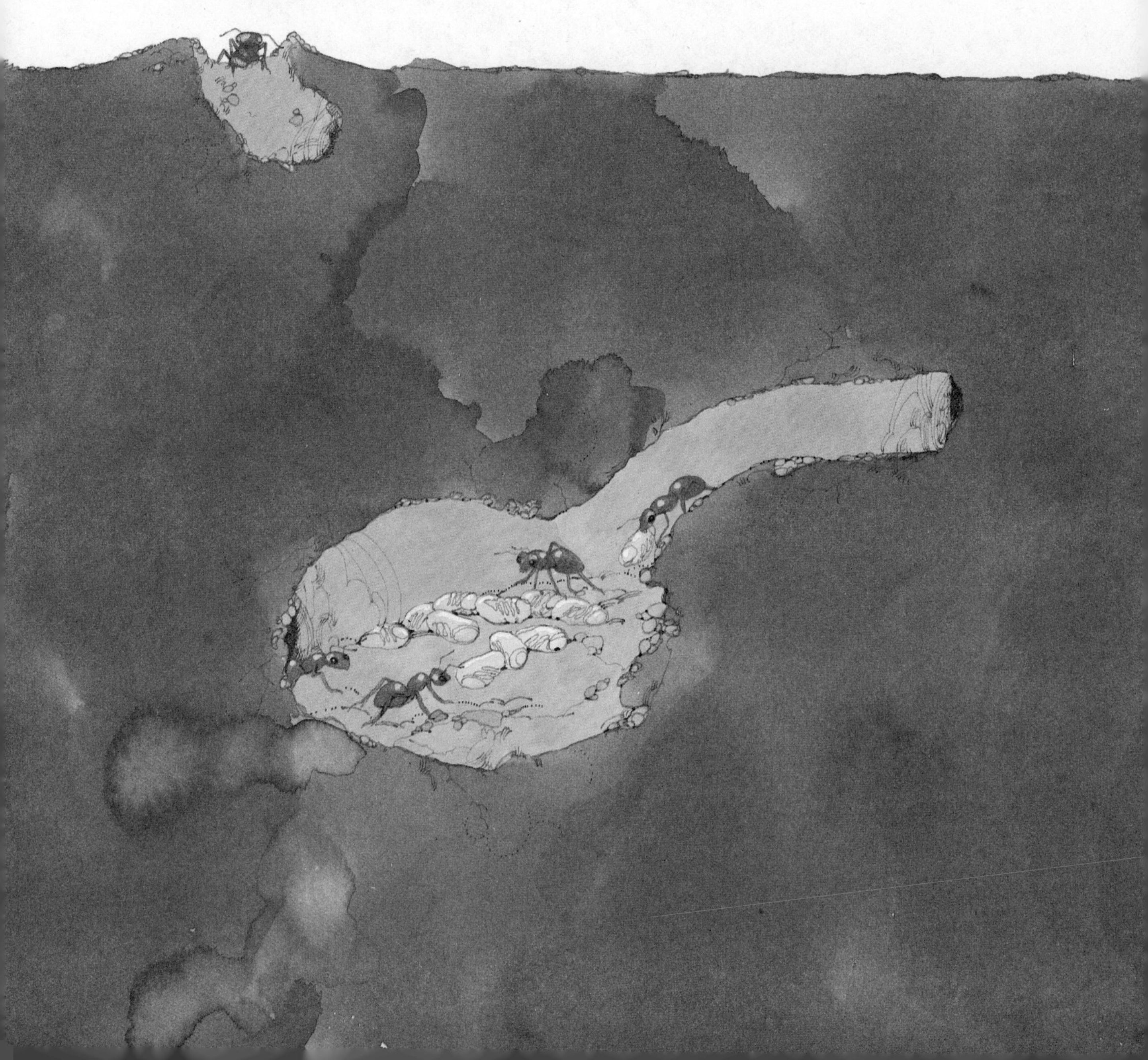

In a month or so, the larvae change into *pupae* (*pyoo*-pee). Worker ants move the pupae to another room. Some pupae look like white ants. Other pupae are covered by white cocoons. Pupae do not eat. But they are still cared for by worker ants. In about 20 days, they are fully grown.

Other rooms in the nest are used to store food. During bad weather, ants cannot go out to find things to eat. So they must have enough stored in the nest.

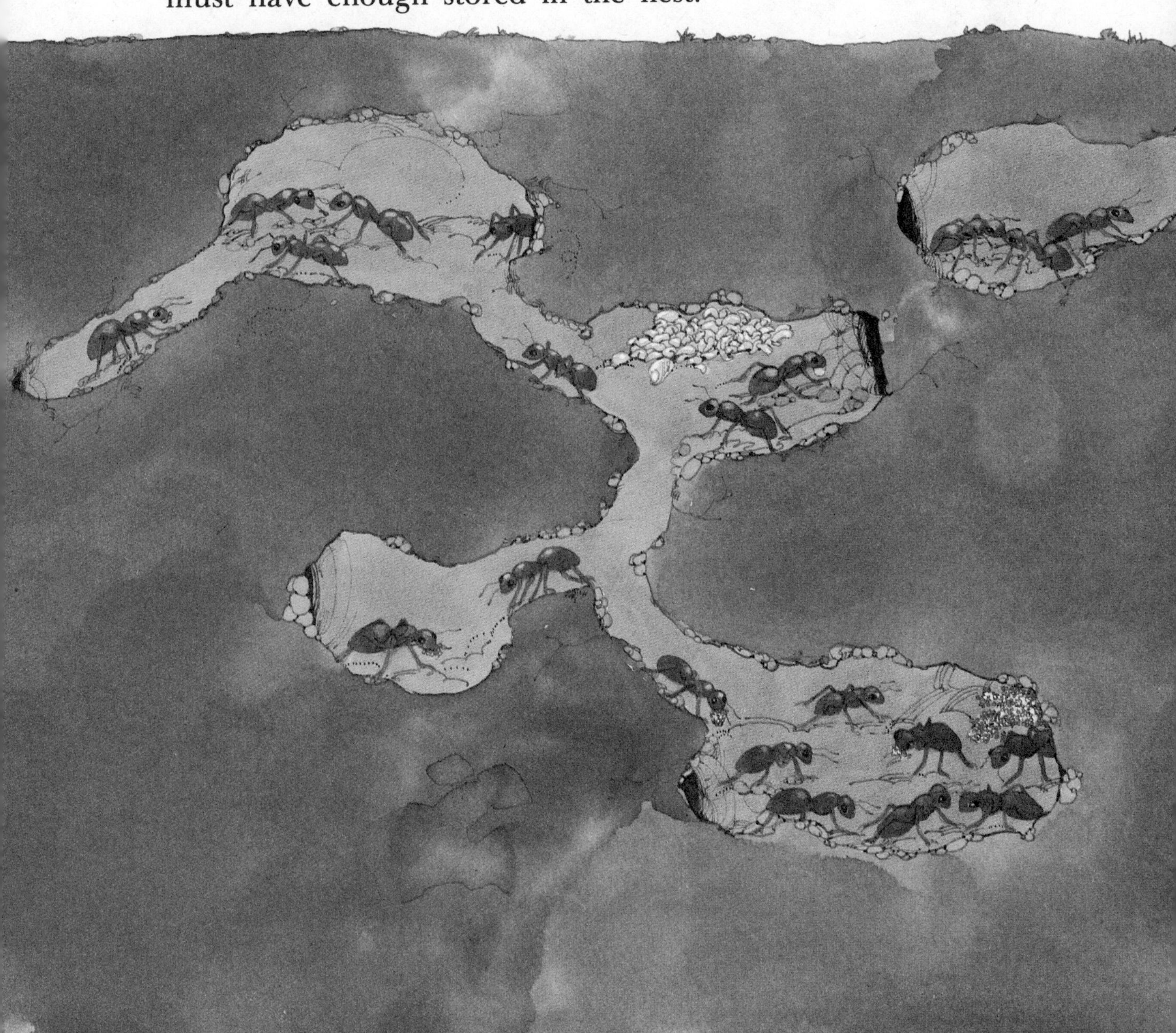

There are other kinds of rooms in the nest. There are rooms to rest in and rooms to sleep in during winter. Ants are always digging tunnels, building new rooms, and closing off rooms they do not want to use anymore.

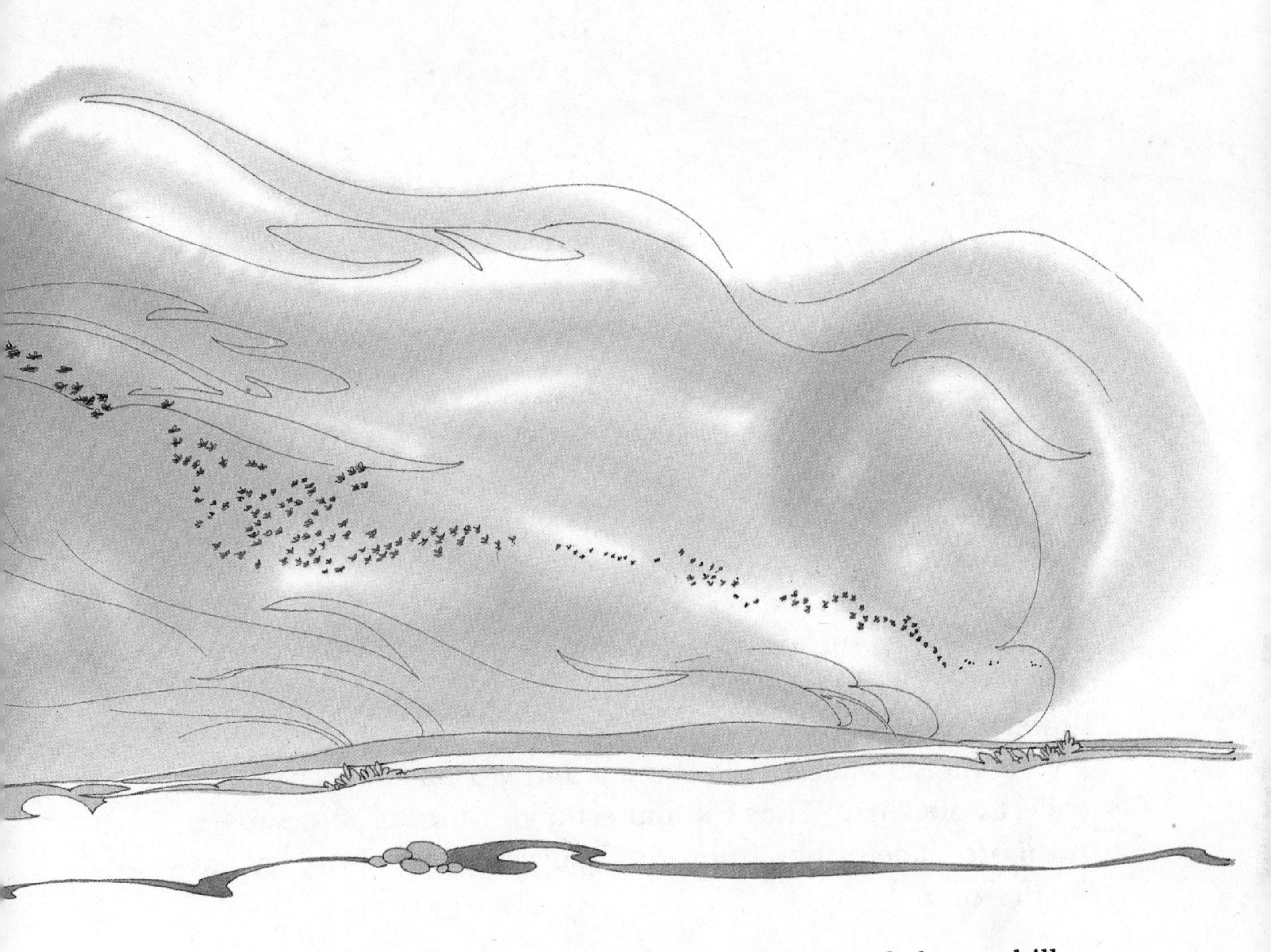

In the spring, ants with wings come out of the anthill. Most of the winged ants are small, but a few are large.

The small ants with wings are drones. The large ones are queens. The drones and the queens mate in the air. Then the queens find places to dig new nests. There, they will begin new colonies. The drones do not return to the nest. Within several days, they die.

There are about eight thousand kinds of ants in the world. Some are large, some are small. Some are peaceful, some are warlike. Ants can be red, black, brown, green, or yellow. But all of them live in colonies, and all ant colonies have a queen.

Honey ants live in the southwest part of the United States. They are found in the desert. A few ants in each colony gather a sweet, sticky substance called honeydew from other insects and plants. They do this just the way bees take nectar from flowers.

At night, some of the honey ants go out of the nest to collect honeydew. They eat and eat and eat, until they can eat no more. Then, they bring the honeydew back to other ants in the nest.

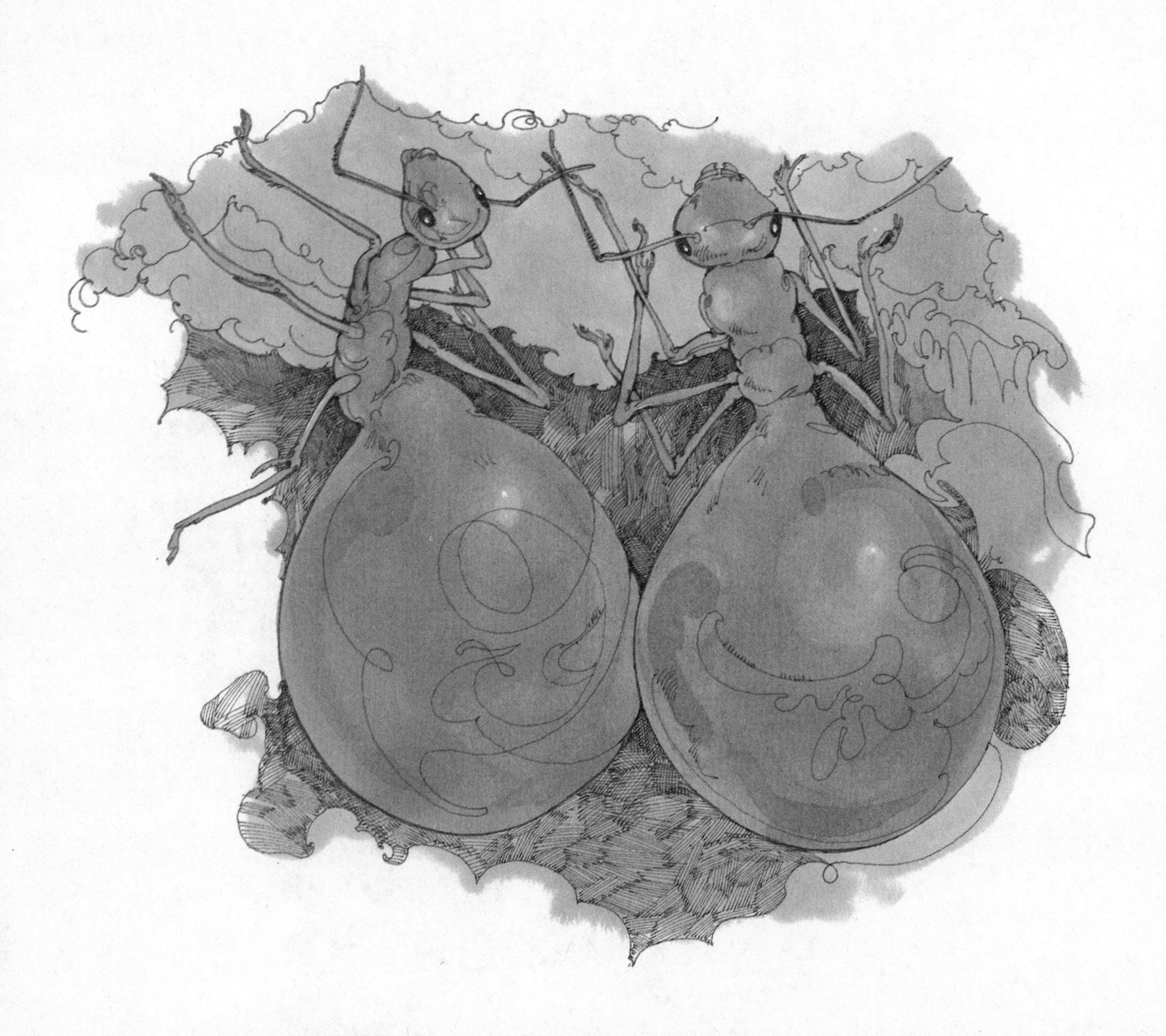

These other ants are special. They store food in their abdomens. They are living storage tanks of food for the rest of the colony. When they are full, their abdomens look like shiny grapes or marbles.

There is a kind of ant found only in Africa and other tropical places. It is called the *weaver* or *tailor ant.* Weaver ants are as green as the leaves they use to make their nests. They sew tree leaves together to form a nest that is waterproof. When it is done, the nest looks like a long, green tube.

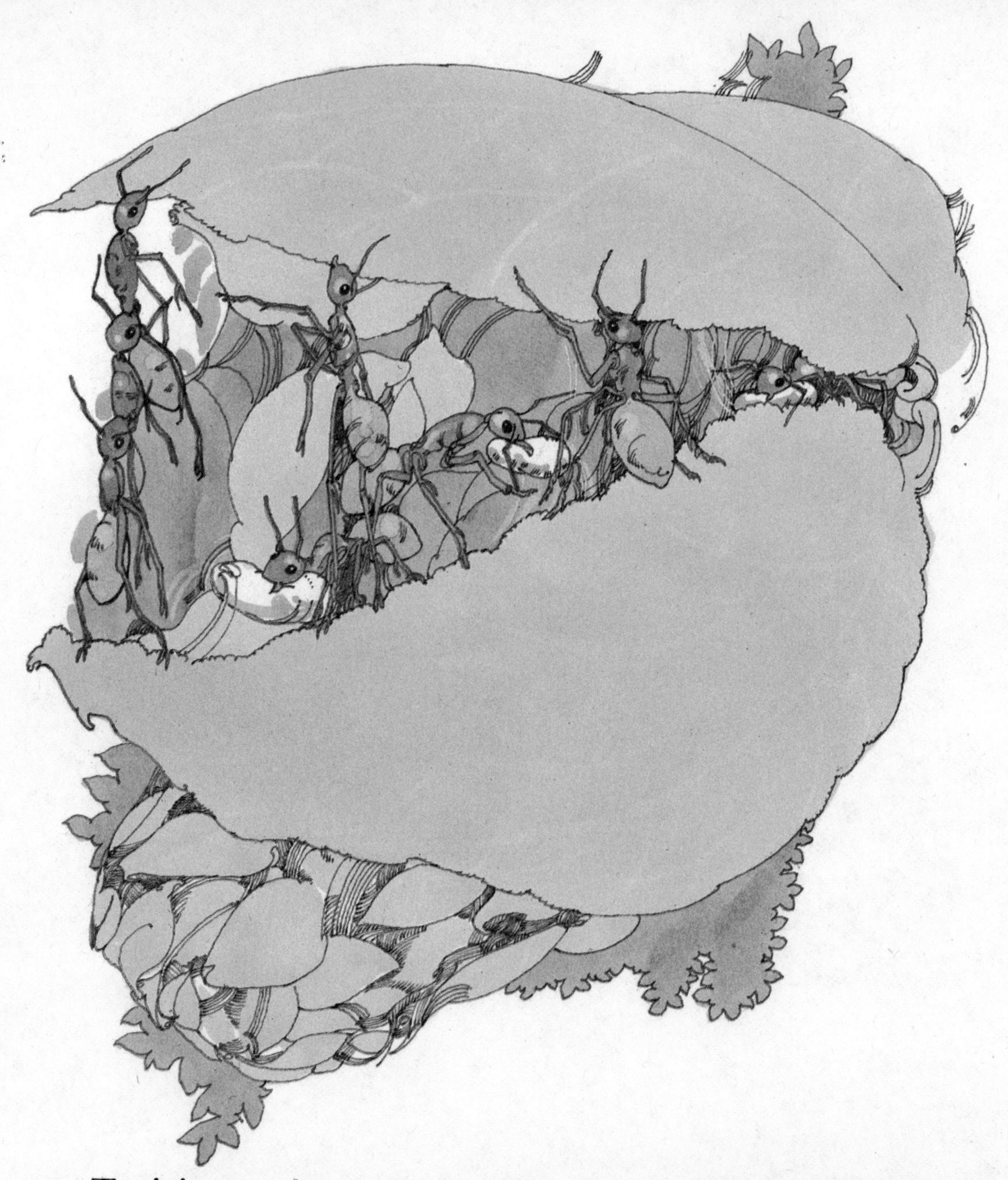

To join two leaves, a few weaver ants hold the leaves' edges together. Other weaver ants hold larvae in their jaws. The larvae give off a kind of silk thread. When a larva runs out of thread, it is put back in the nest. A fresh larva is used in its place.

Some ants are warlike. The army ants of South America and the African driver ants are two of the most dangerous kinds in the world. They eat any insect or small animal that crosses their path.

If you see a leaf that seems to be walking, take a close look. You may find that it is being carried by an ant. This kind of ant is called a leaf-cutter. The leaf-cutter usually works at night. It climbs a tree, cuts off a piece of leaf very neatly, and takes it back to the nest. The ants use the leaves to help grow a fungus that is like a mushroom. This fungus is what leaf-cutters eat.

Leaf-cutter ants work very hard. The leaves they carry back to their nests weigh at least twice as much as the ants. And these ants travel far for the leaves, too. They will go 300 feet, or 90 meters, from their nest to a tree that is 100 feet, or 30 meters, high. That is like a person walking a very long distance and then climbing Mount Everest, the tallest mountain in the world.

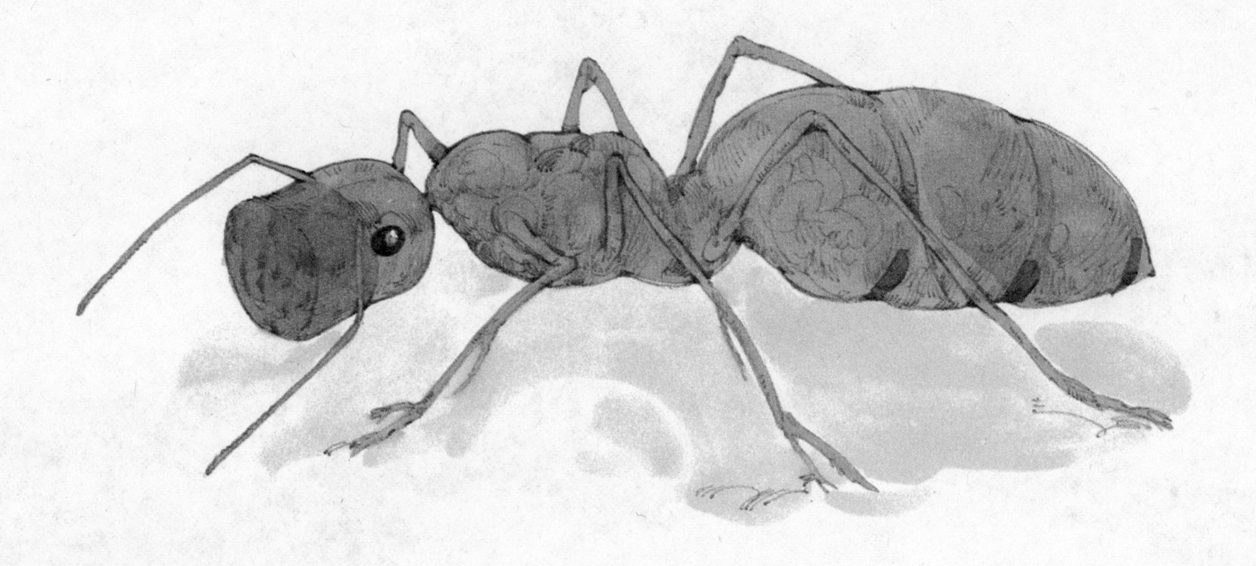

Another odd type of ant lives inside the twigs of trees. Most ants in a twig colony look like other kinds of ants. But a few of the soldier ants look very strange. Their heads are shaped like bottle corks! One of these ants stands guard inside the twig with its flat head in the opening. It acts as a plug.

When a worker wants to come into the twig, it taps the flat head of the living plug. The soldier backs away and lets the worker in. The soldier will not move for anything that does not belong in its nest.

Ants are very strong for their size. Some ants can lift things that weigh 50 times as much as they do. And ants can live on land almost anywhere.

There have been ants on Earth for more than 100 million years! In museums you can see these long-ago ants, trapped in amber. They are fossils. They look just like those uninvited guests who come to your picnics.

The busy life inside an anthill is an amazing one. It is a city filled with six-legged citizens. And in some ways, ants are like people—working together and helping each other to build a community.